My village in the
Sahara

Tarlift,
Tuareg boy

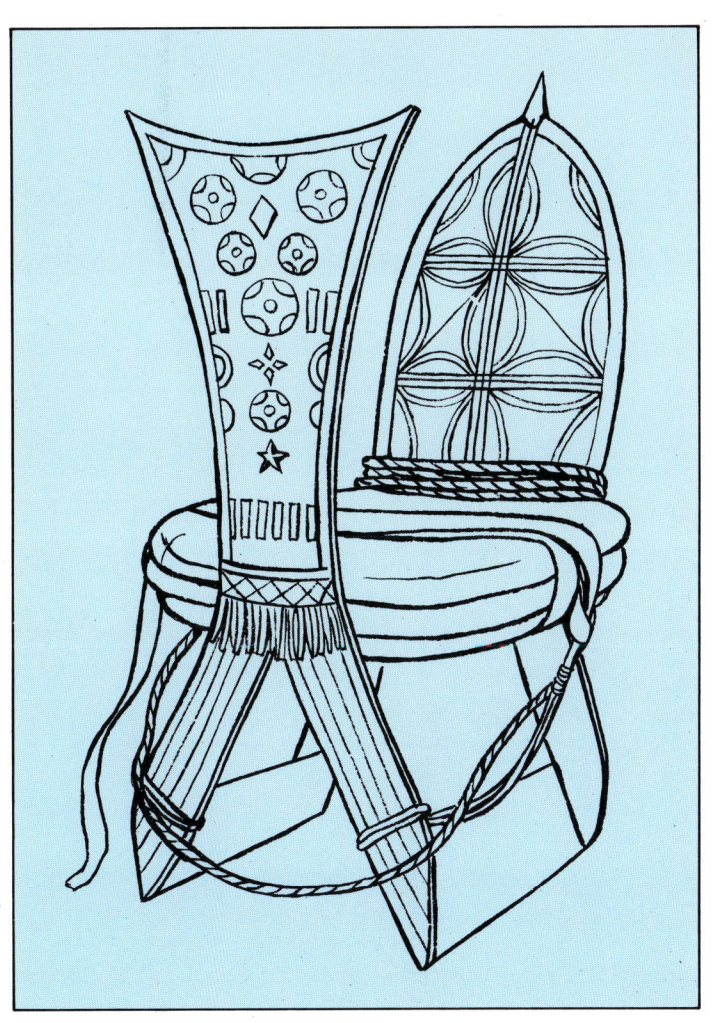

Macdonald

A MACDONALD BOOK

© Librairie Larousse 1983

© English text Macdonald & Co
(Publishers) Ltd 1984

First published in France by Librairie
Larousse as *Tarlift fils de Touareg* with text
and photographs by Anne Rochegude.

Text translated and adapted by
Bridget Daly
Factual Advisor Dr H T Norris
Editor Barbara Tombs

First published in Great Britain in 1984 by
Macdonald & Co (Publishers) Ltd
London and Sydney

A BPCC plc company

BRITISH LIBRARY CATALOGUING IN
PUBLICATION DATA
Rochegude, Anne
Tarlift, Tuareg boy.
1. Sahel–Social life and customs–Juvenile
literature
I. Title
966   DT524
ISBN 0-356-11153-9

Printed and bound in Great Britain by
Purnell & Sons (Book Production) Ltd
Member of the BPCC Group
Paulton, Bristol

Macdonald & Co (Publishers) Ltd
Maxwell House
74 Worship Street
London EC2A 2EN

Contents

MOVING SOUTH

In the great plains of the Sahel, at the edge of the Sahara desert, the season of fertility and fresh green pastures was coming to an end. The Tuareg and their cattle herds were leaving the huge flat plains for the far south, through the already yellowing grasses. The dry season was on its way.

"We and our cattle are in the hands of God!" said Akhaya as he got up that morning. "We must leave now."

Soon the tents made out of animal skins were taken down and carefully folded. Only the wooden stakes were left in the ground; they would be used as firewood by the next nomads who stopped there. Tarlift, Akhaya's son, watched the preparations while he stroked the grey colt.

Akhaya gave the signal to leave and climbed on to his dromedary. In front of him the land seemed to stretch away for ever. He wondered anxiously if the desert pool at Daha, where they were going, would have enough water.

The herd goes south across the great plains of the Sahel.

Akhaya, Tarlift's father, gives the Tuareg the signal to leave.

While the women and servants take down the tents, Tarlift strokes the colt.

4

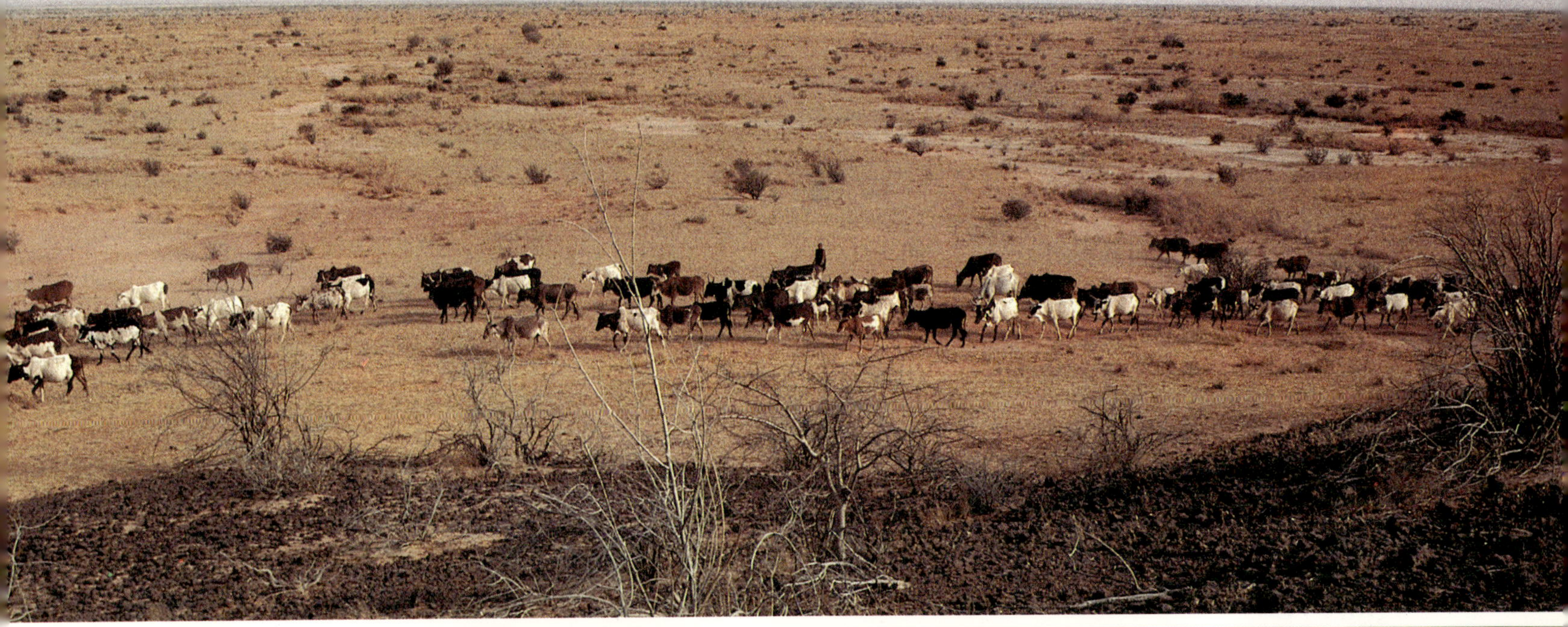

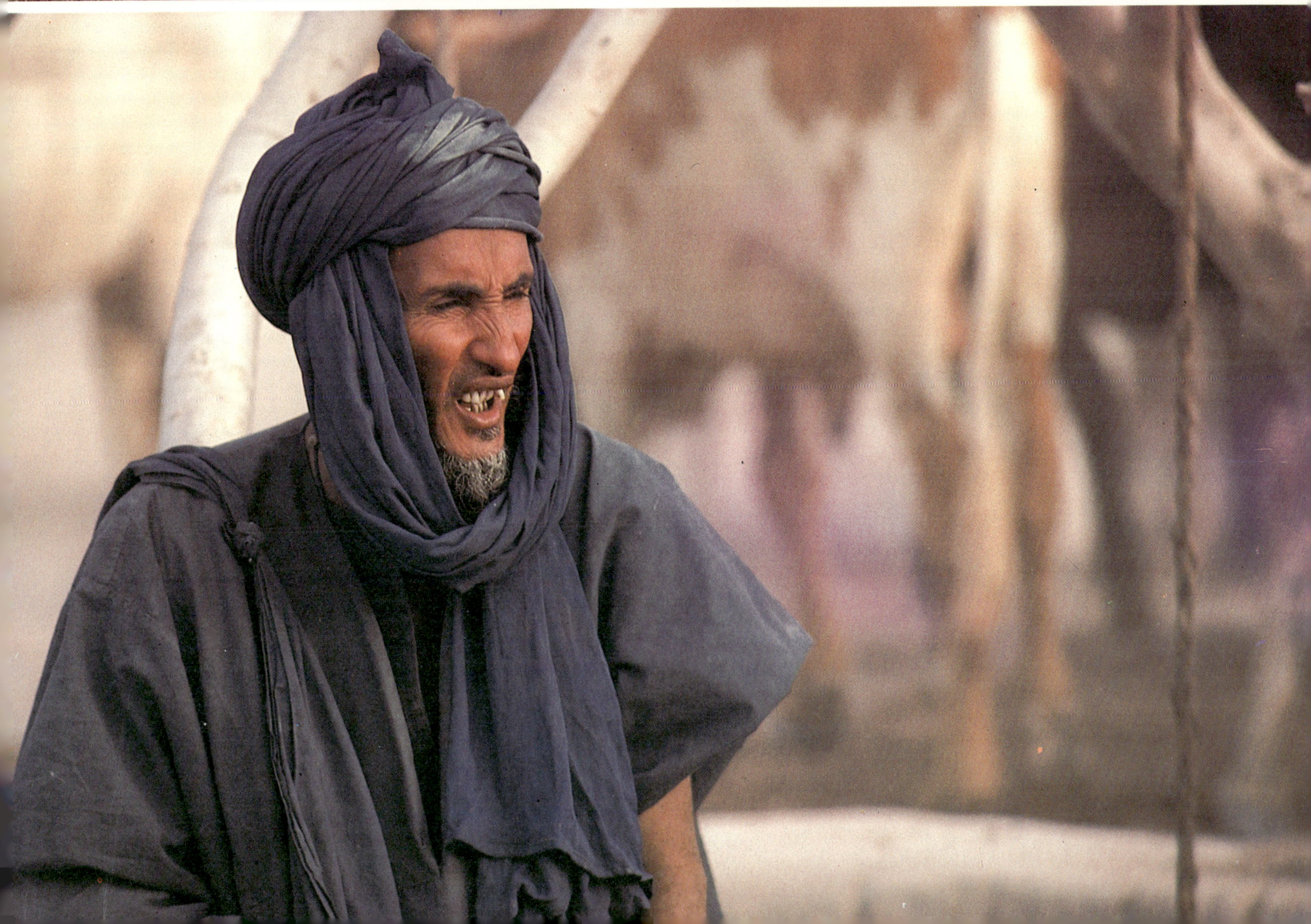

Tarlift makes the journey on foot, beside the cows, or riding on Aoudis, his little pack-ox.

The camp: the tents are surrounded by a circle of thorn-bush branches so that the cows and goats can't get too near; the calves are tied up in front of the entrance.

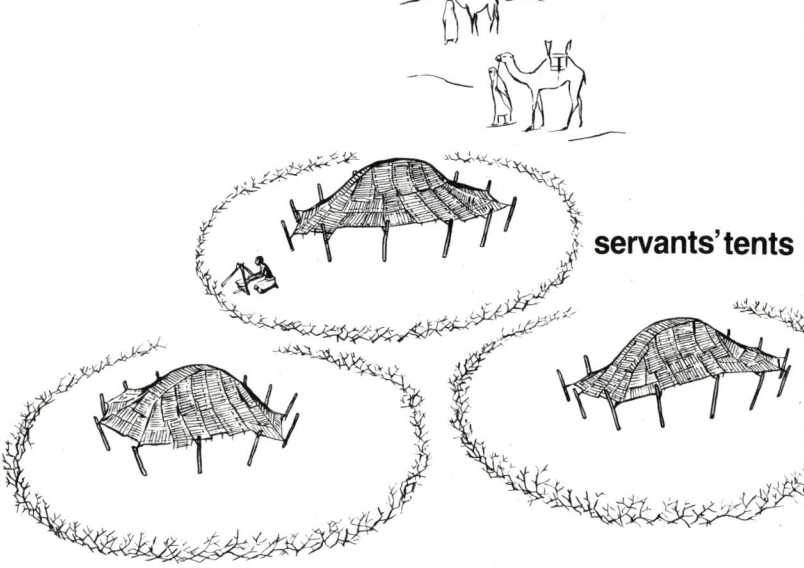

servants' tents

tents belonging to Tarlift's family

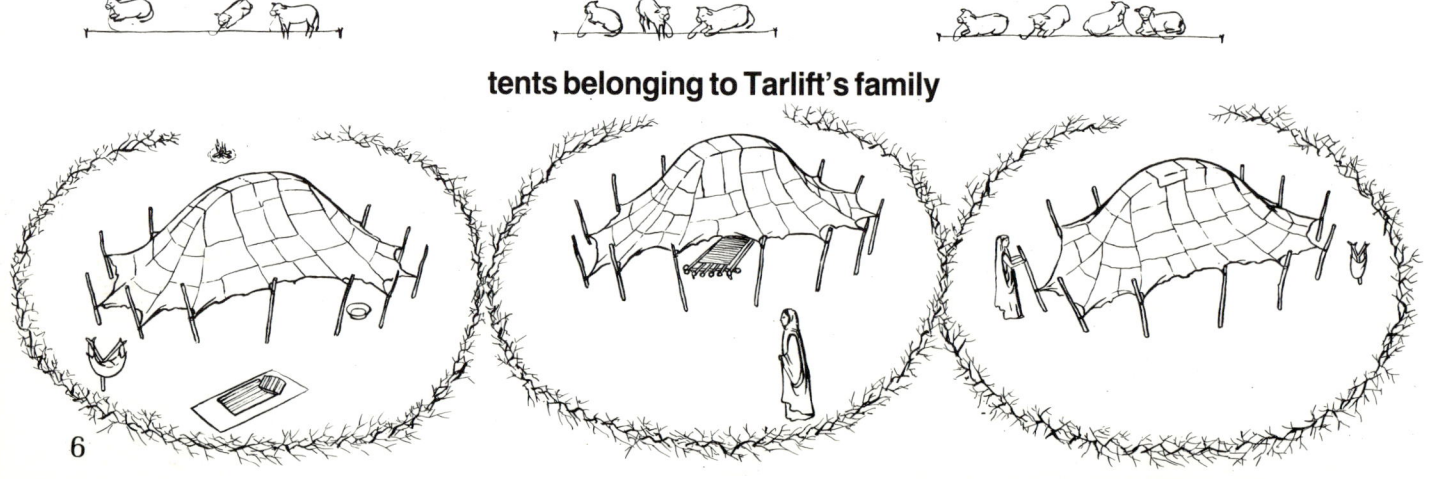

Tarlift went over to his little pack-ox which was licking a leather drinking bottle loaded on the back of one of the donkeys. He took its rope in one hand and in one bound was seated comfortably on its back. His father had given him Aoudis, the little pack-ox, when he had reached the age of twelve.

The men rode at the head of the group, driving the herd of cows. The calves and goats followed a short way behind. The women, riding on oxen or dromedaries, carried their small children and the tiny new-born goats. Donkeys carried the baggage. Tarlift went alone, sometimes riding on Aoudis, sometimes on foot. He was silent except to say the odd word or two to Soumé-with-the-speckled-eyes and Erkech-the-white, the cows which led the herd. If Tarlift slowed down, Soumé would turn her head and wait until he had caught up with her. Then they would continue their long walk together through the dust.

Suddenly a gazelle bounded up and cut across in front of the herd from the right.

"That means good luck!" cried Akhaya. "Good luck goes with us; we shall have water at Daha!"

Thousands of years ago the ancestors of the Tuareg painted pictures of gazelles on the rocks.

The women ride on oxen carrying their children or the baby goats in their arms.

THE DESERT POOL AT DAHA

The sun sloped down towards the earth. The heat became less fierce. Soon the Tuareg and their herds came in sight of the water and the majestic old trees at Daha. The shade of the trees was broad and deep black. The cows had smelled the water well before the men had even seen the trees.

Tarlift herded the calves together and watched them as they drank. Then he tied them to each other in front of his father's tent, which the servants had just finished putting up. Akhaya's camp was made up of five tents. To the west, within shouting distance, were three smaller tents which housed the black servants. Tamou, the little servant girl, and Tarlift's younger sisters had just filled two leather water bottles which they loaded on to a donkey.

The tent: the skins of sheep or cows are sewn together and hung over two arched wooden beams; sharpened stakes are hammered into the ground to hold the edges of the tent in place; the flaps are raised or lowered according to the time of day or the direction of the wind.

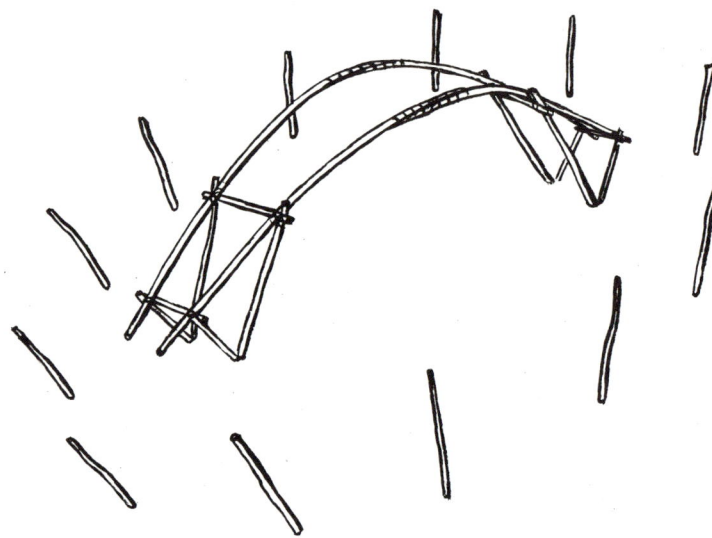

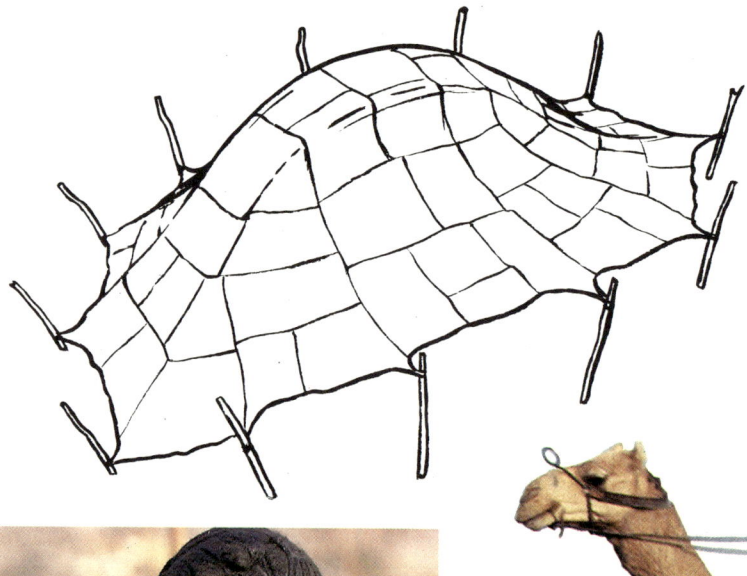

Amina, the servant, churns the milk in a sheepskin bag to make butter.

8

The baby goats are shut in an enclosure of thorn bushes for the night.

Tarlift and Amina's son ride round the water at Daha.

Tarlift trotted round the water on his dromedary. He jumped down quickly to catch the baby goats which had wandered off.

"*Tek! Tek!*" he shouted crossly as he ran, arms outstretched, chasing them in front of him. He ran in bare feet, forgetting the *úzak* thorns which covered the ground. He tripped over some bags, frightening the prized camp chickens, which flapped away squawking, and sent sand flying in his big sister's eyes. She started to chase him. Omar and Amina, the servants, slapped their thighs and shrieked with laughter.

"I'd like to wring their necks!" thought Tarlift as he caught the last two baby goats. He hated looking a fool in front of everyone who was watching him. At last all the kids were chased into their enclosure of thorn bushes.

At dusk the dromedaries come to get their salt which they love licking.

THE STARS COME OUT

Night was only just falling when the herd returned from the fresh pasture, lowing gently. Tarlift's cousin gave the dromedaries some salt. The women and children, sitting in front of their tent, waited for the nicest moment of the day: milking time. Tarlift watched Amina carrying the flaming torch carefully from tent to tent. Akhaya made a hollow in the sand to hold the charcoal. He put some twigs on it and they quickly caught light. A strong, clear flame flared up brightly into the sky.

Omar, the servant, put a large black wooden dish in front of Akhaya. You could hear the froth on the milk bubbling.

"*Amdu!* It's all done!" he said in his firm, deep voice. Omar was so strong that he could fell a tree-trunk with one blow of an axe.

The moon was round and beautiful and shone like a silver dish. Akhaya shared out the milk: one cup for his wife, one for his daughters and the third for Tarlift and his cousins. Seated near the fire, the children were reciting a verse from the Qur'an, to learn it by heart. But Tarlift was daydreaming. He often wandered off to get out of this lesson which the teacher of the Qur'an gave them.

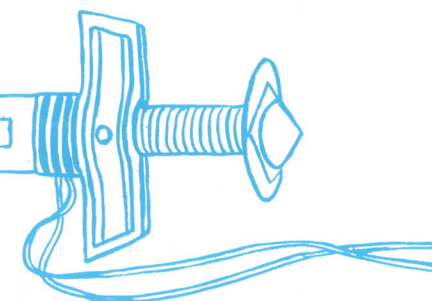

The takouba: a sword with two cutting edges.

Tarlift's secret dream was to go and live with his Uncle Khalid in the big village of Léré. His uncle had told him that he would come and fetch him after the cold season, to enter him at the school. Tarlift remembered the day when he went to the market at Léré with his father. They came into the village on his father's dromedary which was wearing its splendid harness. Tarlift had never seen so many goods for sale: mats, bars of rock salt, sugar, radios, little tea glasses, rubber sandals, torches. There wasn't time to see it all and he hadn't understood everything either, as the people there spoke a different language. Around the market-place the shops were narrow and dark, and the nomads jostled with one another to buy tea.

Tarlift was woken from his day dream by his father.

"Can you see *Amanar*?" he asked his son.

Akhaya was rubbing his teeth with a small stick, leaning his back against one of the tent posts.

"Yes, *abba*. Yes, father, I can see him," answered Tarlift looking up. "I can see his arms too, and his sword, the *takouba*."

"Tarlift," his father went on, "if you look in the direction that the head of *Amanar* and the *takouba* are pointing to, you can see the pole star. It is much brighter than the others. Can you see it?"

"Over there, father, I can see it," said Tarlift, pointing with his finger.

"Over there is the land of the great sand dunes, the land of salt, the north. They say that the animals that we don't see here any longer have gone into hiding in the dunes."

"But there's nothing to eat in the dunes!" said Tarlift, sleepily.

"No. That's why I think that the bustards and ostriches and the herds of gazelle have gone for good now."

But Tarlift wasn't listening any more. Full up with milk, he had fallen asleep next to his father, beside the big empty wooden dish.

The owls called to each other in the silence of the starlit night. The moon watched over both people and animals. The cows chewed slowly, with the wet noses of their calves pressed against their flanks. The goats had joined their kids in the thorn bush enclosure.

Akhaya threw a handful of sand on the fire.

"*Ayyor*, the moon, is the lamp of the night. God has done things well!" he murmured, as he joined his wife and children on the wooden bed in the middle of the tent.

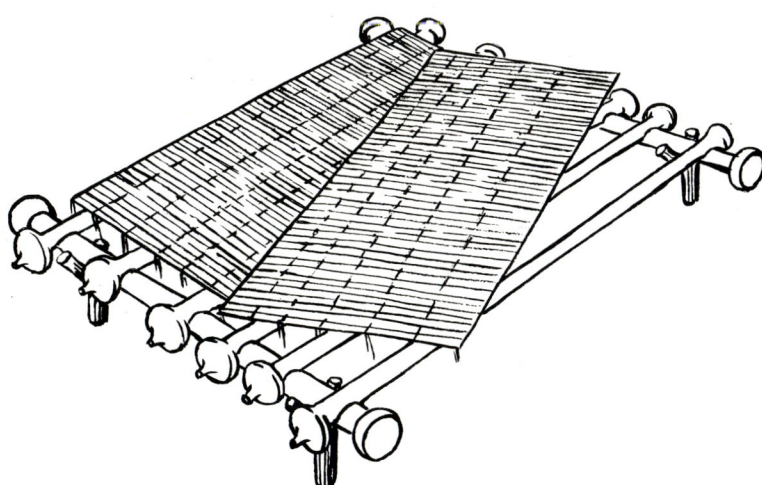

The wooden bed: the slats rest on stakes which hold it away from the ground and insects.

11

TARLIFT LEAVES THE CAMP

"Tarlift! *Enkar! Enkar!* Get up!"

Before he could even open his eyes, Tarlift felt a hand around his ankle and he was being lifted into the air like a rabbit out of its burrow. He found himself hanging upside down. Khalid, his uncle, roared with laughter through the black *taguelmoust* that covered his head and mouth. He let his nephew slip down on to the sand again and sat down beside him. The morning fire was still alight. The men had got up before dawn to pray and now were drinking their first glass of tea of the day and warming themselves by the fire.

Tarlift ties the legs of his uncle's dromedary together, so that the animal cannot wander too far from the tents.

As Tarlift hugged Khalid affectionately he could feel, through the material of his tunic, the stone bracelet that Khalid always wore around his forearm. Tarlift really admired his Uncle Khalid, who came from his mother's side of the family. Like all the men of his race he was tall, proud and noble. He was clever, and had very clear ideas about the problems that made the nomads' lives so difficult. After years of drought, which had caused the death of a large number of animals – and even whole families – Khalid had sold half his herd and bought a house in the large village of Léré. It was there that the nomad animal farmers and the black crop farmers met every week to exchange their goods. Khalid had sent his son Ousmane to school. With Akhaya's agreement he had arranged for Tarlift to go there too so that he could also be taught in French.

Only Tarlift's mother, Mariama, was upset by the sight of Khalid. Silently she sewed a leather bag. She knew that he had come to take her son away. She did not like villages. She preferred the wide open spaces where she had always lived. But she also knew that if Tarlift was educated he could be useful to all of them. And so she had already agreed to Khalid's plan.

"Tarlift, *ma toulid?* How's things?"

"*Elkhir ras,* Khalid. Everything is fine!" answered Tarlift.

Huddled in his brown tunic, he looked at the ground as he spoke to his uncle.

The little flock that Tarlift was given when he was born has doubled in number. Like the dromedaries, goats love salt.

"Go and look at your flock, Tarlift! You might find a newborn kid," said his uncle. Tarlift jumped up and ran off to his animals. His goats, given to him when he was born, were the first possessions that he had owned. The goats were kneeling on the ground, licking a salt bar.

"*Ien, essin, keradh, okkoz,*" he counted quickly. Baawa, Warara and Takachit, his favourites, greeted him with little bleats. Suddenly he discovered a young billy goat which was looking at him curiously.

"What shall I call you, little billy goat?" said Tarlift as he stroked it.

Inside the tent, Khalid touched hands in greeting with the men from the neighbouring tents who came to sit down and exchange news.

"*Isalan?* What's all the news then?"

Khalid told them about the camps he had passed on the way.

"*Elkhir ras.* So things are fine."

He took advantage of his visit to Akhaya to buy four heifers. He would sell them at the next market and with the money would buy rice, tea and sugar. He ordered one of the servants to drive the animals to Léré.

When the sun went down and it became cooler, Khalid asked for his dromedary which had wandered away from the tents to feed on some acacia pods.

Khalid, his face covered by the *taguelmoust,* waits to take his nephew to the village.

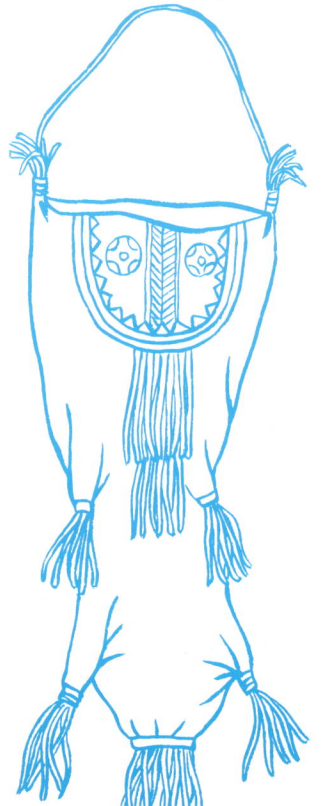

Saddlebag: these leather bags are fixed to the saddle and are used to carry clothes and provisions.

Tarlift stops for a moment to say goodbye to his mother.
Mariama blesses him. Neither shows their feelings.

Bronze padlock: to open it the
key is slipped along, lengthwise.
The women keep the keys
safely, by attaching them to the
end of their shawls.

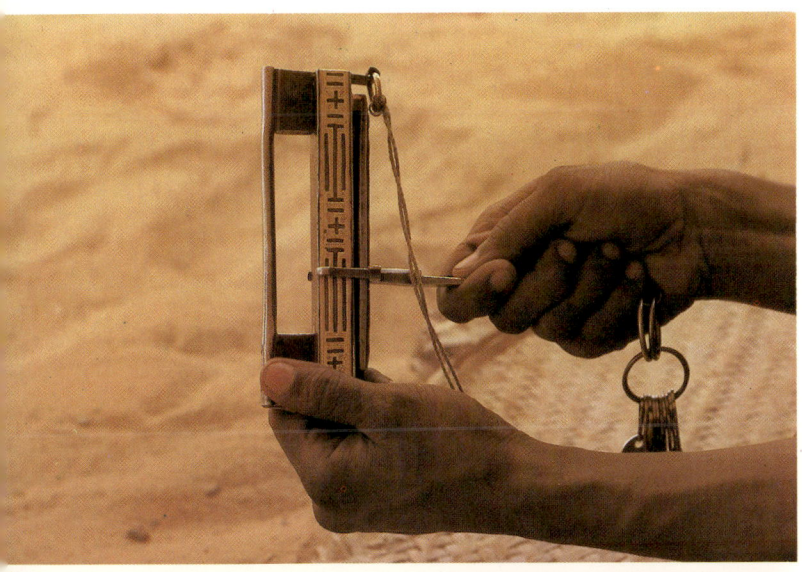

Happy to be going, Tarlift went to say goodbye to his mother. Mariama opened the bronze padlock that closed her bag and pulled out a leather charm which she held out to Tarlift. She put the good luck token around his neck. Her son would be protected now. While she blessed him, Tarlift held his mother's cool hand. He knew that he mustn't show any feelings. He jumped up and walked away towards his father and uncle, holding his head high. He turned his back on the tent, his goats, the water and his sisters. He said goodbye to Akhaya and climbed up on to the dromedary behind Khalid. He didn't have any baggage, because he didn't have anything to take.

When they had gone, it was very quiet in Akhaya's tent. The only sound was the feeble bleating of the newborn kids, and the murmur of Mariama praying as she watched the outline of the dromedary disappear over the horizon.

Lucky charm: Tarlift's leather charm contains a verse from the Qur'an.

15

The saddle: the wooden frame is covered with leather dyed in bright colours and held in place with bronze nails.

THE VILLAGE, AND HOMESICKNESS

Several weeks later, in Khalid's house, Ousmane was serving the tea out under the watchful eye of his sister, when a strong wind started to blow.

In minutes the entire village vanished under the clouds of sand whipped up by the wind. The villagers only just had time to take cover in the nearest house.

"There'll be sand in the rice again," thought Tarlift gloomily.

"*Adou*, this wind. I like the wind in the open desert – I don't like it in the village."

He looked at Khalid's tent, which had been folded up and put away neatly with the carved stakes. Khalid's rifle was hanging on a nail, above the pale green leather saddle studded with copper.

The wind died down as quickly as it had risen, and Ousmane had to remake the tea. Sitting next to his uncle, Tarlift thought about school. He was new and was just beginning to understand French. There were no books, and the mud and straw hut was very hot because it had a corrugated iron roof.

A violent sandstorm suddenly blows up. In the village of Léré, the people take shelter in the nearest house.

In Khalid's house, his daughter drinks a bowl of milk while Ousmane prepares the tea.

But Tarlift loved geography lessons. He had just learnt that the Earth was round; in the camps the men said that the Earth was flat and surrounded by water. And he had never realised that there were so many countries. He wondered whether everyone else on Earth had herds of cows and goats, and what they fed their animals on where there were no *úzak* or acacias.

Sitting on the ground, Ousmane watched the tea which was boiling gently on the charcoal fire. When he had finished serving it out, he slid over to Tarlift like a cat.

The village football team. Tarlift is standing, third from the right.

"Hey Tarlift! *Io!* Come on!" Ousmane whispered to him.

"*Ma imous?* What is it?" asked Tarlift.

"There's a football game over by the dromedary market."

Tarlift got up and the two boys slipped out. In the courtyard, Khalid's wife was washing her baby in the sunshine.

Ousmane was the team captain and he had let Tarlift join because he was a fast runner. But, in spite of being used to his long walks with the herds, Tarlift came away tired out from these football matches played in the burning sand and the hot sun.

At the end of the day, lorries arrived bringing the traders to market in the square. At the first sound of the engines, the game broke up. The lorry drivers, looking worn out, climbed down from their cabs, followed by their apprentice mechanics. The passengers, numb from their long ride, shook the dust from their tunics. At the moment, Léré's market-place was only a heap of materials, sacks of grain, ropes and matting. In the narrow streets, the huge lorry wheels stirred up clouds of sand. The children, excited by the thought of the weekly market which was going to take place the next day, ran up to old Dembélé's lorry.

"Hey, what's the news?" asked Tarlift.

"Have you seen my cousins?"

"Yes, Tarlift, your cousins all say hallo," replied old Dembélé. "They are all fine."

And old Dembélé went back to work, selling tickets to the passengers who wanted to travel back with him the day after the market.

Tarlift was secretly very happy:

"Tomorrow I'll go up on the roof of Khalid's house. I'll be as quiet as a lizard and I'll be able to see the nomads arriving from all the corners of the horizon," he thought to himself.

That night, Tarlift felt sad. This sadness, which he felt every time he thought about his camp, seemed to be growing as time went on. He really wanted to leave the village for good. Around the brazier where the tea was brewing, tall black-shaped figures had come to sit silently with Khalid. Their soft voices rose in the darkness. They each gave the news from their own camp and from those they had passed on the way. This was how Tarlift learnt that his father had gone to Mauritania with his eldest brother, to take him to a Moorish doctor. He was the only one who knew which herbs would cure bad chests and coughs.

Tarlift felt a lump in his throat when he heard his father's name spoken. He drew away from the circle of men and put his straw mat down in a corner to go to sleep. But he wanted to leave so much that he couldn't sleep. He had a nomad's blood flowing through his veins, not a villager's. Thinking more and more about leaving, he waited until *Amanar*, the large and beautiful constellation, rose in the sky. He looked up at the warrior with his legs and arms of shining stars, found the sword and followed the direction it pointed in, northwards to the pole star.

"There's the north. They're all there, Soumé-with-the-speckled-eyes, Erkech-the-white, my baby goats and my father's colt."

The last visitors had left Khalid's house. The tame sheep bleated far into the night. When dawn broke, Tarlift knew that he would leave.

In the sunshine, Khalid's wife washes her baby which lies on the little servant girl's knees.

Old Dembélé drives his lorry into the village.

19

THE SALT TRADER

Tired out by the bustle of the market, where he had been since school had finished, Tarlift went to sit down by the salt trader. He was cutting up the enormous bars of rock salt that had been carried on the backs of dromedaries from the desert salt works. The Tuareg could not do without tea, salt or sugar. So Tarlift was certain to meet at least one of the men from his camp at the salt trader's. He didn't have to wait long. Zeddou arrived, and as they talked Tarlift learnt that his camp had stopped at the wells near to the Mauritanian frontier, a full day's dromedary ride from Léré. Akhaya was coming back soon, with his elder brother who was well again. Tarlift asked for news about everyone and everything: his mother, his sisters, the servants and the animals. Tired of all these questions, Zeddou said laughingly:

"Aren't you enjoying it here then? Don't forget, you're going to learn a lot, you'll be able to do multiplication, to count all the animals and work out how much to sell them for!"

Tarlift, his eyes fixed on the ground, didn't answer. No, he wasn't happy any more. *Ténéré*, the open desert, was calling him – its pull was stronger than ever. Here the wind didn't have the same smell of freedom. There were too many people and not enough milk. He couldn't fight with his sisters or have dromedary races. He had seen enough market days – more than four now.

"Tomorrow I'll follow the tracks of Zeddou's dromedary," thought Tarlift, as he wandered off to see his friend the little tailor. "I'm going to walk to the camp. I shall find the wells. *Insh Allah!* God willing! I want to see the gazelles again and the wild guinea fowl. I don't want to live shut up in a house any more. *Eglir!* I'm off!"

The following day, the little tailor was the only person in the village who knew Tarlift's secret. The stars in the constellation of the camel had only just faded. In the east, a pale blue light showed that dawn was breaking. A cock crowed. Tarlift got up very quietly. One of Khalid's sheep watched him. Tarlift gave it a branch to chew, to stop it bleating. Then he quickly put on his sandals and his tunic and slipped out into the alley.

The sound of voices came from the last few houses in the village: Tarlift thought he wouldn't have to wait long for Zeddou to come out. He hid among the market dromedaries and kept an eye on the northern road out of the village. He waited, but nothing happened.

"But Zeddou never drinks tea before he goes out!" thought Tarlift angrily.

The village was waking up. Donkeys started to bray, the dromedaries roared, the dogs ran about excitedly and flies settled on anyone they could see. The sun was already warming the earth. Tarlift counted the dried dates that he had taken with him: one handful, eight dates. Suddenly a group of nomads went past Tarlift without seeing him.

The little tailor is a Targui like Tarlift. He won't tell anyone Tarlift's secret.

He just had time to recognise Zeddou. His dromedary was trotting quickly. Tarlift saw the flash of the copper nails in his saddle and the sheath of his *takouba*. He waited a few minutes and then ran out to find the tracks, clearly marked in the sand which had become firm in the cold night air. He set off.

Some black and white *moula-moula* birds flew up singing, telling the news of Tarlift's journey. Tarlift knew that he had to walk a long way. To give himself courage, he held on tightly to the bird-trap that Ousmane had given him.

The salt trader cuts up the bars of rock salt carried from the northern salt works on the backs of dromedaries.

Aïcha, the old blacksmith, reads the signs in the sand.

AÏCHA'S PROPHECY

Meanwhile at Akhaya's camp, Mariama and Tarlift's sisters were making buttermilk with the servant girl. Mariama was thoughtful. That night she had dreamt that a baby camel had walked towards its mother. But it had walked in the wrong direction, away from the wells and the water-holes. Then she saw her son's face and didn't know where he was. She could not forget her dream.

Mariama got up and draped her blue shawl around her shoulders. This meant that she was going to visit one of the neighbouring tents. Saying hallo to everyone she met on the way, she went over to Aïcha's tent. Aïcha had so many wrinkles that she looked very old. She put down the leather bag that she was sewing and invited Mariama to sit down on a leather cushion.

The two women exchanged the usual greetings. Mariama picked off the prickly *úzak* burrs from the bottom of her skirt, showing a calmness she didn't feel.

"Aïcha, I want you to read the signs in the sand. I had a bad dream. Ask the sand where Tarlift is," Mariama said.

The old blacksmith hid her face in her shawl. Above her head, the skin tent hung in rags. With her piercing eyes, she looked at Akhaya's wife. Their families had known each other for so long that everyone had forgotten when they first met. With a quick gesture she swept the sand. With her first and second fingers she made marks like animal tracks. She drew seven rows, then rubbed them out.

"Your son isn't at the place where he slept last night," she said.

22

"Your son is walking, but in the wrong direction," she says to Mariama.

She drew another set of marks.

"He is walking, but the wrong way."

Mariama shivered. Aïcha traced a third set of marks. Then she swept the sand quickly and kept her eyes lowered. She did not dare say what she had just read.

"Tarlift is in God's hands," was all she said.

Mariama slipped her a Malian hundred franc piece and with a heavy heart returned to her tent. She knew that Aïcha, the blacksmith, wouldn't tell her any more.

For two days, Tarlift walks across the vast sandy wastes and rocky plateaus, looking for his camp.

TARLIFT'S LONG WALK

For two days Tarlift walked, sometimes over plateaus where only shrubs grew, sometimes over large sandy wastes. Animals ran away as he came near. Wild guinea fowl flew up from under his feet. Tarlift walked confidently because he remembered the migration routes. His instincts were sharpened by years of the family migrations, northwards to the salt lands or southwards when grass and water began to dry up.

He didn't feel at all frightened and only stopped to rest when the sun was too hot. Then he found the shade of an acacia tree and swept a bit of sand free from insects and prickly *úzak* seeds. Then he dozed, with a stick close beside him to defend himself.

He remembered a pool in the clay soil of a small valley where he could quench his thirst. On the way he had picked some *jujube* berries, all the time following Zeddou's tracks. He passed through an endless countryside of grasses and thorn bushes. The earth stretched away for ever and the sky above was a vast blue expanse. Then the soil became firmer and Tarlift crossed a rocky plateau.

The red stones slipped under his feet and he grabbed on to the grey stems of the euphorbia bushes. They had a white, sticky sap. At the hottest time of the day, when hares lay still in their forms, Tarlift became uncertain about which way to go. It was time to rest but Zeddou's tracks had disappeared among the stones. So Tarlift looked at the tufts of grass to see if he could see any that had been flattened by the dromedaries' hooves. He retraced his steps patiently, but he couldn't even find his own footprints.

The sun was high in the sky and the grass looked white in the burning heat. In the camp, a few hours walk away, his mother couldn't stop seeing her son's face, nor Aïcha's. Akhaya wasn't there to advise her. "Perhaps the blacksmith read the sand wrong!" she said to herself.

Worn out by the heat, Tarlift slid into the shade under a thornbush and left fate to decide his future. He hardly noticed the flock of turtle doves rise into the sky as he fell asleep.

When he woke up he tried hard to remember which plateau he was on.

"*Ounan,* the wells. Where are they?"

The desert grasses became tinged with orange as the sun went down. To pass the time and to forget his tiredness, Tarlift took the bird-trap out of his pocket and set it up in a hollow in the sand. He watched the red globe of the sun going slowly down. When he looked at the trap again, a lovely turtle dove was fluttering wildly, trying to release its trapped foot. Tarlift killed it quickly, already thinking about the smell of roast meat. He collected some twigs, took his precious matches out of his pocket and lit a fire. He added a piece of sun-whitened wood to the fire and blew softly.

He fixed the plucked turtle-dove to a straight branch which he stuck in the sand above the fire. The night had closed in without his noticing. A little gerbil, attracted by the firelight, hopped up. They both stopped and stared at one another. Then, its curiosity satisfied, the gerbil turned and disappeared amongst the stones.

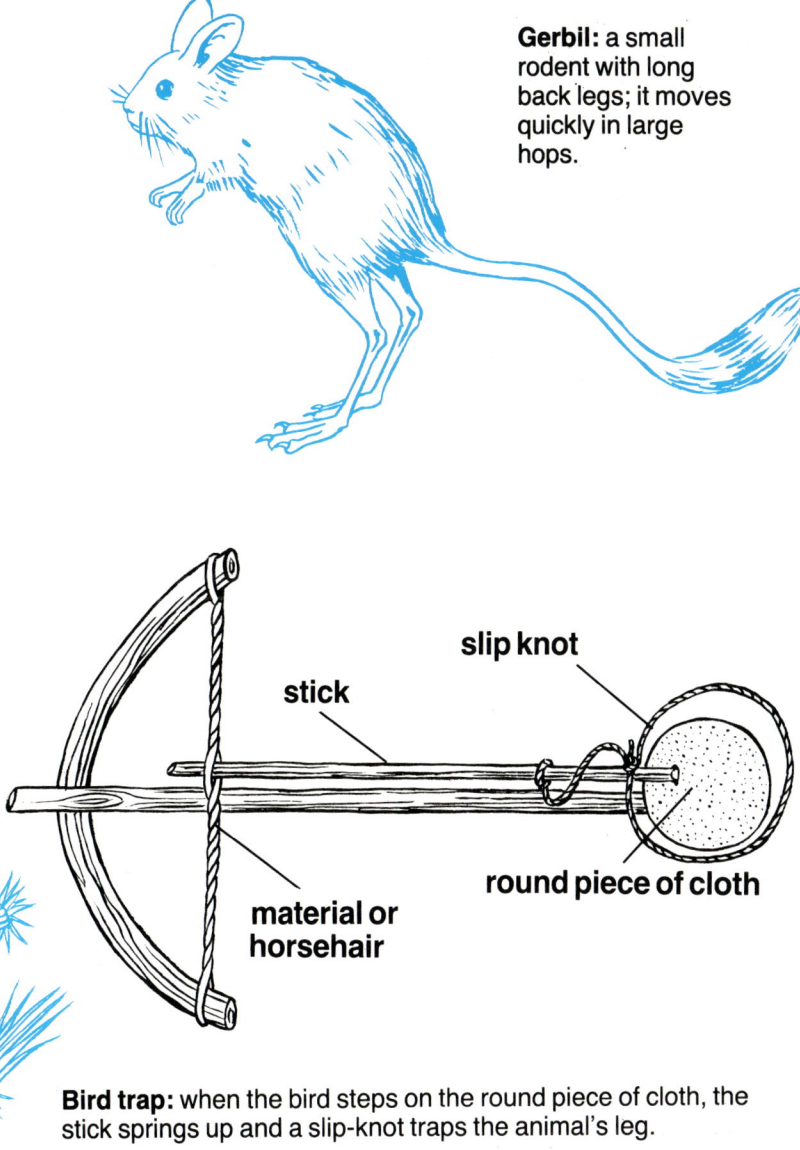

Gerbil: a small rodent with long back legs; it moves quickly in large hops.

slip knot

stick

round piece of cloth

material or horsehair

Uzak: a little grass-like plant whose seeds are covered by a case protected by thorns. The *úzak* sticks to everything and the thorns are difficult to get out of your skin.

Bird trap: when the bird steps on the round piece of cloth, the stick springs up and a slip-knot traps the animal's leg.

Amanar: *Amanar,* the warrior, is the constellation of Orion which we can see quite clearly on winter nights in Europe. His sword points towards the north.

After resting, Tarlift digs out an ants' nest to find the ants' grain store.

THE WARRIOR OF THE SKY

A chill wind blew from the north, sweeping down from the high dunes and carrying some of their sand with it. It crossed the wide plains, shook the acacia trees and pushed the thorn bushes in front of it. Tarlift, his hunger gone, found a strip of soft sand to lie down on. But he couldn't sleep because he was shivering with cold. He took three smooth stones and put them on the fire. When they were warm, he slipped them next to his body and wrapped himself in his tunic, tucking it over his head. Then, curled up like a hunting dog, he slept at last, under the pale round moon.

Several hours later, he woke up with a start, feeling that there was something there, although he couldn't hear or see anything. Wondering if it could be the *effri*, the wicked spirits of the desert, he took out his little knife and stabbed at the air in front of him to fend them off. Then, reassured, he looked up at the stars and the moon. *Amanar,* the sky warrior, shone above him. Slowly he began to remember his father's words:

"The herds move in the direction of the setting sun towards the water-hole and the red hill, then towards the north to the wells of Akhor."

Tarlift looked at *Amanar,* and found the sword and the head of the sky warrior. Suddenly his nomad's instincts were revived. He knew now that the wells were to the north in the direction that *Amanar* pointed to. He looked into the far distance by the cold light of the moon. Suddenly he caught sight of a pale glow. His heart leapt.

"Perhaps it's a camp fire," he thought. He set off. His feet didn't feel the cold or the *úzak* spikes. He walked until dawn, and then all through the morning. He was thirsty and dreamt of cups full of frothy milk. When he sat down under a tree to rest, he saw a long column of ants. As he watched where they went, he found their nest and remembered the stories Amina, the servant, would tell. In times of famine, the families looked everywhere for ants' nests. When they began to dig with their hands they found, to their delight, the ants' store of grain. By the wide river Niger, they piled up the wild grain. Tarlift dug in his turn and gathered several handfuls of grain.

"How am I going to eat it?" he thought, "I can't cook it. Still it's better than nothing."

He laughed at the indignant ants, scattered by his digging, and wrapped the grain in a corner of his tunic, securing it with a knot. Near him a huge dung beetle was pushing a round black ball.

"At least he knows where he's going!" thought Tarlift, setting off again.

27

THE WELLS OF AKHOR

Several hours later, Omar, the tall servant, was most surprised to see his young master running towards him. He nearly let go of the rope he was holding and let the bucket fall down the well again. Tarlift ran towards him and Omar took his small hand in his own large rough one.

"Are you at peace?" he asked.

"Yes I am," replied Tarlift.

"Where have you come from, little traveller?" asked Omar, laughing.

"I've come from Léré," said Akhaya's son.

Omar shook his head in disbelief.

"Enta da! He's here!" shouts Tarlift's little sister as she runs towards the camp.

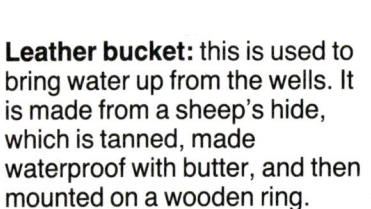

Leather bucket: this is used to bring water up from the wells. It is made from a sheep's hide, which is tanned, made waterproof with butter, and then mounted on a wooden ring.

Tarlift arrives at the Akhor wells. "Where have you come from, little traveller?" asks Omar, the servant.

Back in his tent, Tarlift is happy to be with his mother again. He is tired out from his long walk.

Soon all the people who had driven their herds to the wells gathered around Tarlift. The cows lowed because all their drinking troughs were empty.

"*Ekfid aman.* Give me some water," begged Tarlift. "I haven't had a drink for such a long time."

Assou, his little sister, skipped round him shouting his name, thrilled by the idea that they could soon begin their fights again. Then she flew like the wind to their tent.

"*Enta da, enta da!* He's here, he's here!" she cried in her squeaky voice.

The servants stopped work and Mariama stopped praying. Mataïssa, his eldest sister, put her baby down and laughed with joy. Everyone got up to look at Akhaya's youngest son. The bottom of his tunic was covered in *úzak* burrs and the expression on his face showed how glad he was to be back.

He went up to his mother, lay down, and put his head in her lap without a word. Mariama did not show how happy and relieved she was. For three long days she had believed her son to be lost or dead, and now here he was near to her again, safe and sound.

Tarlift shares in the meal with the menfolk of the camp: rice tossed in melted butter. The spoons are wooden and carved with geometrical designs.

Tarlift carries the long bundles of grass to the dromedaries...

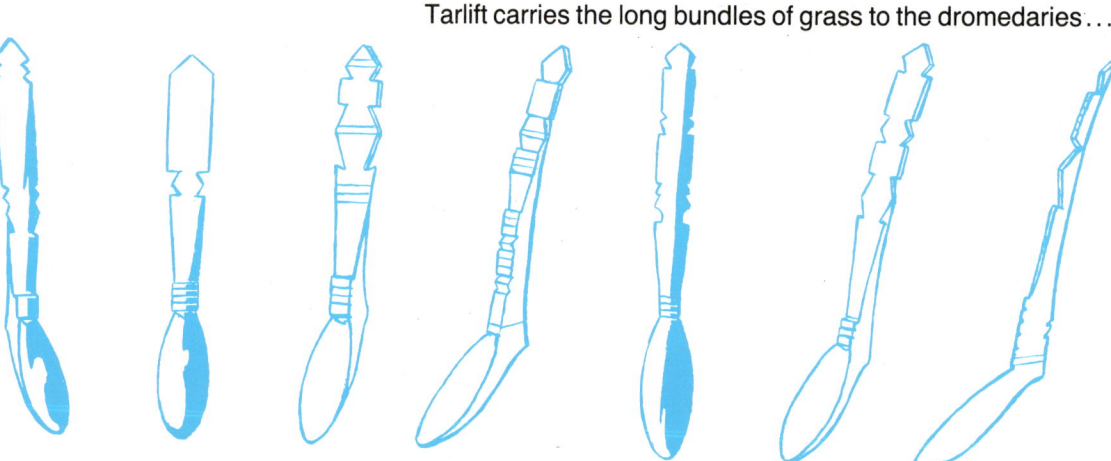

The servants had lit a fire a short distance away. They were preparing the daily meal, a huge pot of rice which would be divided into three: some for the men; some for the women; and the rest for the servants. That day Amina put a lot of extra melted butter in the men's rice.

Tarlift soon took his place again in camp life, but he was afraid that his father would be angry when he found out that he had left school and Khalid's house. He willingly made the tea when asked and did much more work than before. Their camp was close to an area where some very tall grasses grew. Every year, Mariama took the chance to weave some new mats and repair the old ones. Tarlift, his elder brother and two of the other men from the camp went to cut the grass. They trotted off on their dromedaries to the shady corner where the grass grew straight and tall.

They tied up their mounts and began to cut the grass stems at the base of the tufts. Then they tied them in bundles and piled them up. Tarlift worked as hard as the others in spite of the heat. Then came the most difficult part: loading up the dromedaries. The first one, scared by the sight of the huge bundle that the men were trying to attach to the saddle, reared up suddenly and galloped off, scattering everything in its path.

A streak of white sprinted after it. Tarlift's elder brother, his teeth clenched and his eyes burning with anger, chased the rebellious dromedary.

At last they finished loading up and the little group headed back to camp. There was an unusual amount of bustle going on. Two dromedaries were tied up in front of Tarlift's tent. Who did they belong to? Who were the visitors?

...then he returns to the camp.

AKHAYA'S RETURN

Akhaya, Tarlift's father, had come home after several weeks away. All the nomads came to welcome him. His brother was well again and the musicians had been called. Their clear voices rose into the sky. Accompanied by an instrument similar to a lute, they sang the praises of Tarlift's ancestors, of their noble souls and pure blood. Mariama and Mataïssa had brought out their best mats. They clapped their hands in time to the music and a delicious smell of roast meat wafted into the tent. It was very hot. There was no breeze in the tent which had been warmed by the sun. Lounging next to each other the nomads exchanged all their news.

"How's things?"
"How's the herd?"
"What's the grazing like?"

To celebrate Akhaya's return, one of the musicians, his face hidden in his *taguelmoust,* sings the praises of the family ancestors.

"Tarlift, people don't talk about serious things when they have just arrived home," says Akhaya to his son.

Tarlift didn't dare get down from his dromedary and waited for a signal from his father. None came. Tarlift knew that he had been wrong to leave the village and he felt ashamed. Mariama looked on silently.

At last Akhaya looked up at his son.

"Tarlift."

"Yes, *abba*? Yes, father?"

"I don't want to talk about serious things when I've just arrived home."

"No father."

"Didn't you meet any jackals or hyenas?"

"I only heard the jackals barking during the night."

"And how many days did it take you to get here?"

"Three days, father."

Akhaya laughed.

"Well, I'm not going to let you drive the animals to market yet! They would have all died of thirst before you'd found the road to the village! But you were brave. You want to stay with us. Well, God's will be done! But, since you've chosen this way of life you must make sure you study the Qur'an every day!"

Tarlift knows that he has done wrong and doesn't dare get down from his dromedary.

Tarlift left the tent. Everyone had heard what Akhaya said. Tarlift would stay with them. He was happy and knew that now he would learn the verses from the Qur'an without grumbling. He accepted the rules and would keep to them.

He helped to cut up the second sheep that had just been killed for the feast. Then they carefully grilled the liver. It was the best bit and they took it to Akhaya's brother, who shared it with the others. When the sheep was roasted, Tarlift took a piece and rubbed it with the bar of salt which was being passed round. The musicians took up their instruments again and began to sing about ancient battles between tribes or against the French. Tarlift wandered off and went to give a handful of millet to the colt. Its coat had got thicker. He stroked its grey mane and whispered,

"Little horse, when you grow up, we'll go up to the red hills where I slept all alone."

Tarlift has put a large helping of millet in the colt's nosebag.

The sheep has just been killed. Tarlift and his cousin cut it up before roasting it.

LIFE GOES ON

The weeks passed. Tarlift studied his verses from the Qur'an. Sometimes a young Qur'an teacher would make him recite them. Mataïssa corrected her younger brother's writing board.

"It is God who has given you the earth for a bed and the heavens for a roof.

It is he who makes the rain fall from the skies to make the crops grow and become food for you to eat."

A young teacher of the Qur'an copies out a passage.

In the shade of a euphorbia tree, Tarlift and his cousin learn the verse that they will have to recite.

The verse is written in ink on wooden slates, and is rubbed out when it has been learnt.

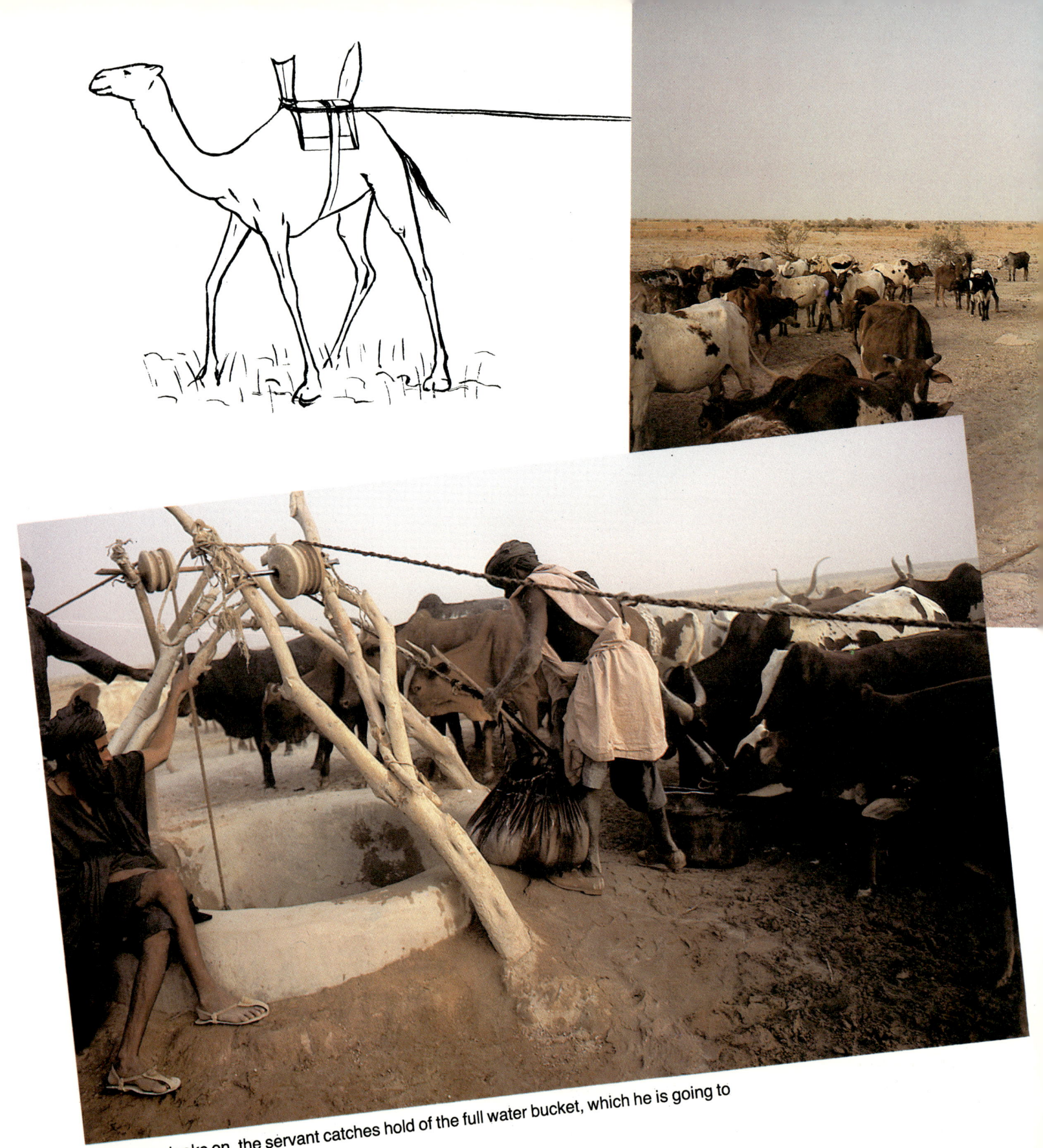

As Akhaya looks on, the servant catches hold of the full water bucket, which he is going to empty into the drinking trough.

Tarlift steadies the pace of the dromedary which has just pulled the bucket up, by pulling on a rope fixed to its saddle.

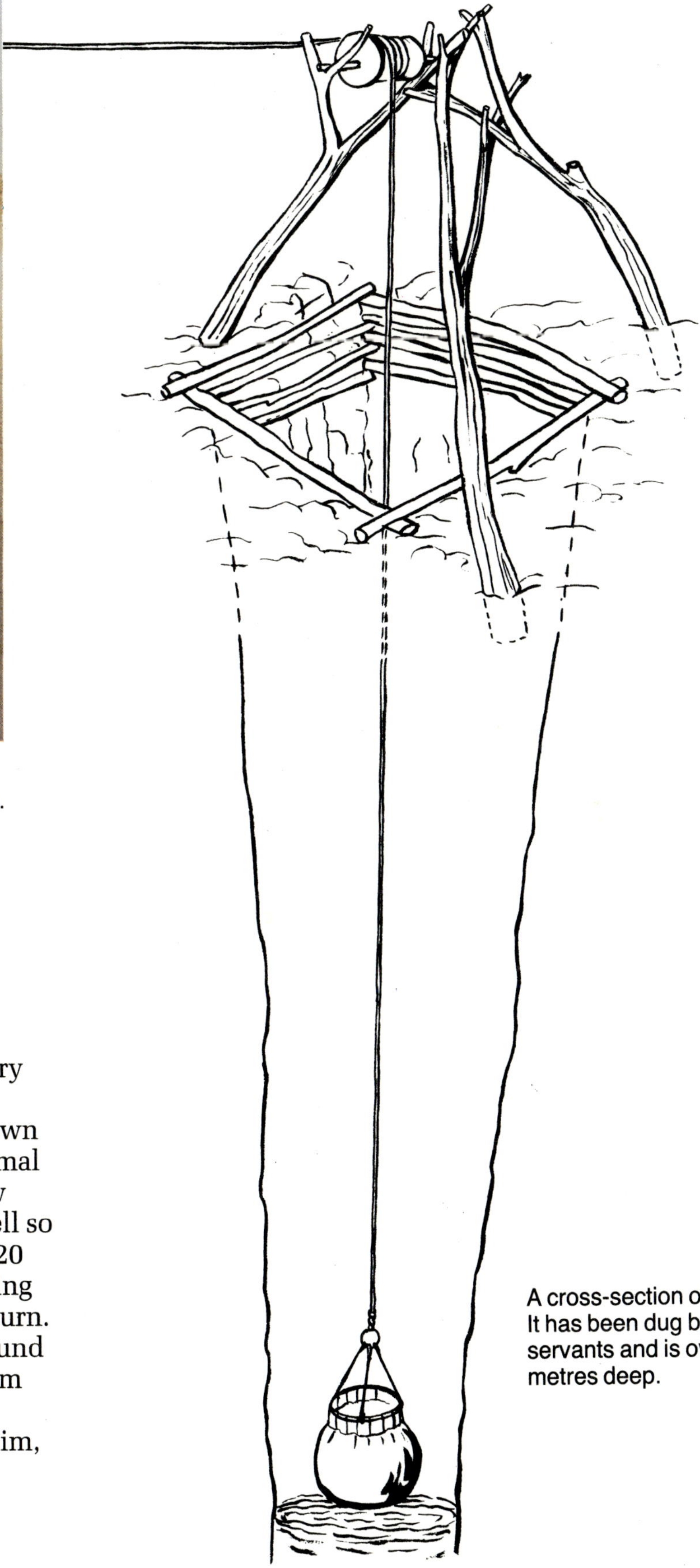

Omar taught him how to make a dromedary run in a straight line to raise a bucket from the bottom of a well. The water level was going down and the rope was over 60 metres long. The animal had to move at a steady pace and it had to slow down when the bucket reached the top of a well so that someone could catch hold of it. Then the 20 litres of water would be thrown into the drinking trough. The herdsmen waited for their herd's turn. The cows lowed in the white dust that flew round them. When he recognised one of the cows from the herd, Tarlift called out to it. Soumé-with-the-speckled-eyes came over to him, while Erkech-the-white looked at him.

A cross-section of the well. It has been dug by the servants and is over 60 metres deep.

39

The months pass. Every morning Tarlift leads the cows to pasture.

The months passed. Akhaya's camp moved on from place to place, always travelling further south. Ever since his long walk, Tarlift was almost treated like one of the grown-up men. He looked forward to the time when he would be able to wear the *taguelmoust* around his head.

"Not for several seasons yet though," he sighed.

At night when the herds returned from grazing, Tarlift walked to the wells with his father. The cows came back later and later because they had to go further afield to find grass. Akhaya watched his son grow up; he was proud that he showed so much strength. Soon Tarlift would be allowed to milk the cows. A tent was added to the camp, belonging to old Ishaka, the Qur'an teacher.

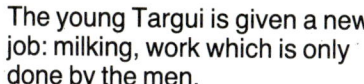

The young Targui is given a new job: milking, work which is only done by the men.

Every day Tarlift joins his cousins in the tent belonging to old Ishaka.

He wanted to go back up north with Akhaya, when the rainy season began. From then on, Tarlift joined his cousins every morning in the old monk's tent. So he went on with his studies of the Qur'an but was not separated from his family nor the animals. As for Mariama, she decided it was time that Tarlift began to learn how to write in *tifinar*, the alphabet of the Tuareg people.

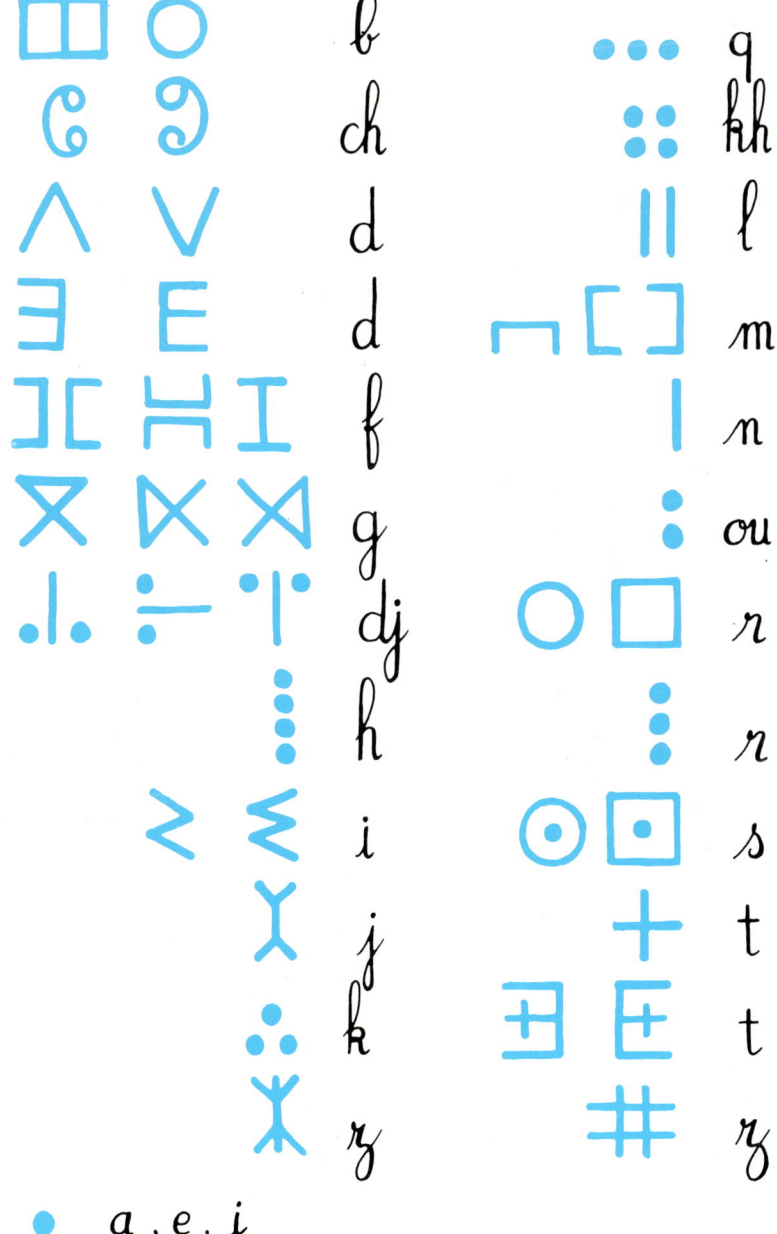

In the evenings, Mariama draws the letters of the *tifinar* alphabet in the sand for her son.

GLOSSARY

The people

Tarlift
our hero, 12 years old
Akhaya
his father
Mariama
his mother
Mataïssa and Assou
his sisters
Khalid
his uncle from Léré
Ousmane
Khalid's son and Tarlift's cousin
Omar and Amina
the servants
Tamou
their daughter
Zeddou
a Targui from Akhaya's camp
Dembélé
a lorry driver from the south
Aïcha
the old blacksmith
Ishaka
the teacher of the Qur'an

The animals

Soumé-with-the-speckled-eyes,
Erkech-the-white
Tarlift's favourite cows
Baawa, Warara and Takachit
his goats
Aoudis
his little pack-ox

The places

The desert pool at Daha
The village of Léré
The wells of Akhor

Vocabulary

Abba
father or dad
Adou
the wind
Amanar
the sky warrior (Orion)
Amdu
It's all done
Anou
a well
Ayyor
the moon
Effri
wicked spirits
Eglir
I'm off
Ekfid aman
Give me water
Elkhir ras
Everything is fine!
Enkar!
Get up!
Enta da!
He's here!
Euphorbia
a tree with a smooth grey trunk and a white sticky sap
Ien, essin, keradh, okkoz
one, two, three, four
Imda!
It's finished!
Insh Allah! (Arabic)
God willing!
Io!
Come on!
Isalan?
What news?
Jujube
a bush with berries the size of a small olive which are both sugary and acid and which children like sucking

Ma imous?
What is it?
Ma toulid?
How are you?
Moula-moula
little black and white birds which bring good luck
Ounan
the wells
Takouba
a sword
Taguelmoust
head-dress worn by the men
Tek!
a sound made to drive the animals along
Ténéré
the open desert
Úzak
a sort of grass which has seeds protected by thorny spikes.

Pronunciation

W is pronounced like our 'w'.
R is sometimes pronounced like our 'r' and sometimes at the back of the throat like 'ch' in German.
There are different pronunciations in different areas.

THE SAHEL

Sahel, in Arabic, means 'shore'. The Sahel is like the shore on the edge of the desert. This long belt of desolate land stretches across West Africa from the Atlantic to Lake Chad. It is the semi-arid steppe country at the edge of the Sahara desert, separating it from the Savanna. It is inhabited by nomadic peoples and by some crop farmers. To the north, in the steppes, acacia and thorn bushes grow as well as the grass which feeds the herds. To the south stretches the large expanse of grass and flood plain of the Niger valley.

THE SAHEL COUNTRIES
Mauritania, Senegal, Mali, Upper-Volta, Niger, Chad.

POLITICAL SYSTEMS
Republics.

POPULATION
Of the 25 million people in the six countries, 6 million live in the Sahel.

CURRENCY
The CFA franc (10,000 CFA francs = £20), except for the Malian franc (10,000 Malian francs = £10).

LANGUAGES
The official language is French, but each community has kept their own language; Tamashek, Peul, Hausa, Hassāniyyah Arabic etc.

RELIGION
Muslim with a small minority of Christians and a few traditional African religious communities.

CLIMATE
Tropical with a very low rainfall. A cold season from November to March. A hot season from April to October. If the rains come, they fall from 15 July to 31 August.

TARLIFT, TUAREG BOY

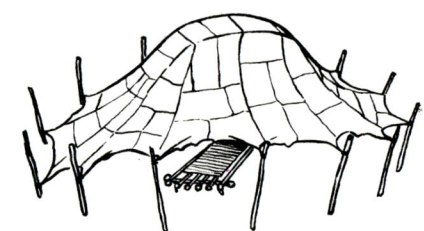

Tarlift is a Targui
Targui is the singular of Tuareg (Targuia for a girl). Tarlift belongs to one of the numerous Tuareg tribes who live in the Sahara and the Sahel. They all speak the same language, *Tamashek*, and have the same customs, with a few regional differences. Their alphabet is *tifinar*.

The origins of the Tuareg
The Tuareg are of Berber origin. The rock paintings and carvings found in caves in the Sahara are evidence of pastoral peoples who lived thousands of years ago. Later people from Fezzan in Libya spread south towards the river Niger, settling in the Tassili, Ahaggar, in the Aïr Massif then in the great plains of the Sahel.

Why are they nomads?
The Tuareg are continually on the move according to the seasons, to find water and pastures to feed their herds. They shelter in tents which are made out of skins and are easy to carry. For a long time they were fierce warriors and lived by demanding taxes from caravans which crossed their territory and by raiding enemy tribes. Nowadays they exist by raising cattle, using the main resource of the Sahel – grassland. The cattle are sold when necessary to buy rice, sugar or tea.

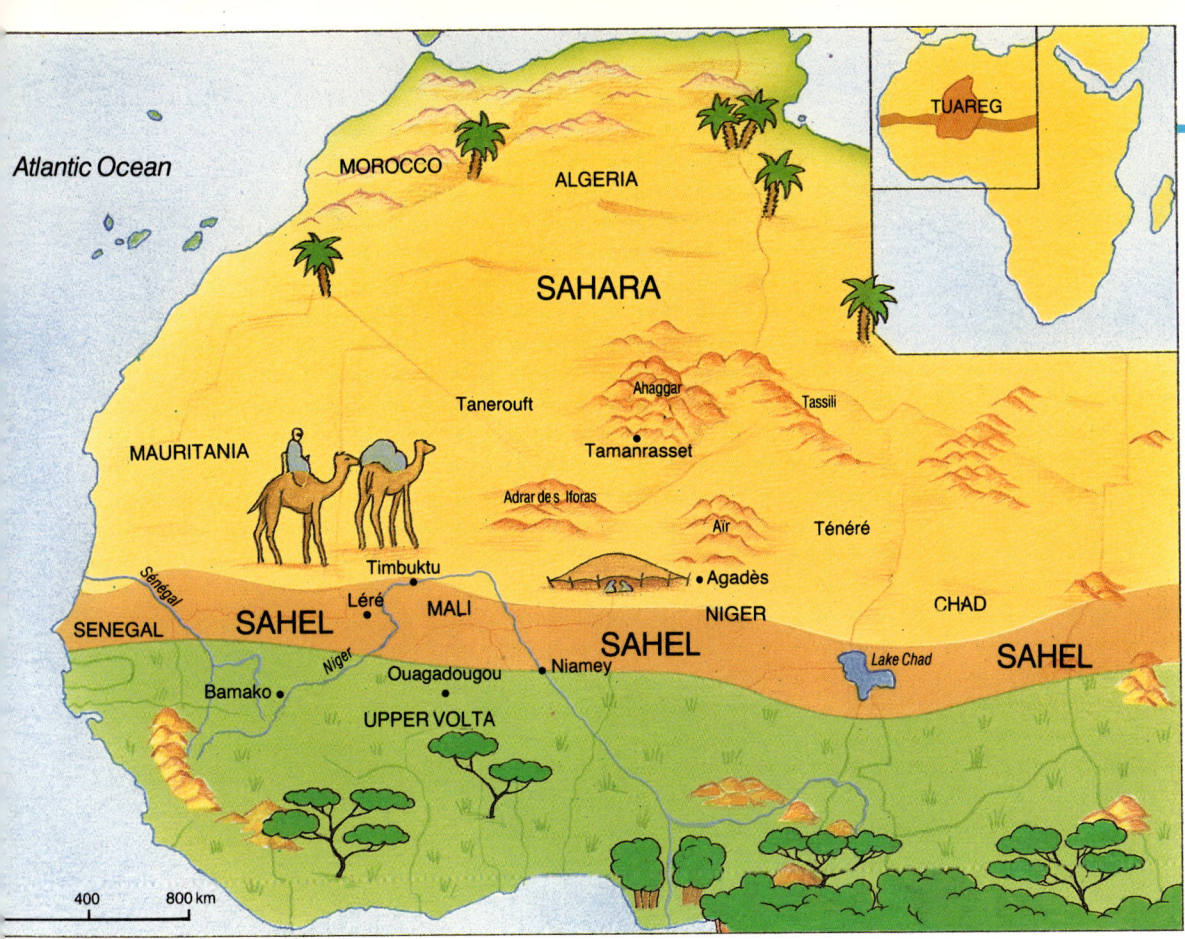

How is their society organised?

The society is structured as follows:

1) the tribesmen or 'free men' (warriors, vassals and teachers of the Qur'an)
2) the artisans, smiths and musicians (the men work in wood and metal, the women in leather)
3) the buzus or freed slaves who stay in service of their own accord. (Since 1930 there are officially no more slaves.)

The nobles have lost their absolute power. Today the head of a group (a tribe is divided into smaller groups) is also an administrator, responsible for collecting taxes for the government.

The taguelmoust

This is a long veil or scarf (from 6 to 9 metres long) which the Tuareg wind around their heads. It also covers the lower part of their faces because a Targui must never show his mouth in public.

The *taguelmoust* has two uses: it is protection from the sun and it is also a mark of respect for others. The indigo blue *taguelmoust* is the most popular, but it is a very expensive material which comes from Nigeria. The dye stains the skin. That is why the Tuareg are called "the blue people".

The Qur'an

The Qur'an is the Muslim holy book. It has 114 chapters, called *sūras*, divided into verses. It is the word of God told to Mohammed by the archangel Gabriel. God's message is that a series of prophets have been sent to reveal how people should live in order to gain their reward in paradise. The Qur'an forms a basis of Islamic law. It is taught by a scholar teacher, called an *Anislem*. The Arabs brought the Muslim religion to the Tuareg around the 11th century.

The dromedary

The dromedary, or Arabian camel has only one hump, whereas the Bactrian camel has two. Its call is known as a "roar". It originally came from Arabia and was introduced into Africa when the desert began to spread (about 2000 years ago). In the cold season it can go for about 500 km without water. Its training starts when it is grown up at five years old, and continues for several years.

47